Verses & Lyrics

Verses & Lyrics

by Zishan Evans

Artwork by Reynaldo Logrono.
Cover design by Victor La Gambina.
Book design by Printed Page Productions, Berkeley, California.

Order this book online at www.trafford.com
or email orders@trafford.com

Most Trafford titles are also available at major online book retailers.

Print information available on the last page.

ISBN: 978-1-4120-9315-6 (sc)

Trafford rev. 08/13/2018

www.trafford.com

North America & international
toll-free: 1 888 232 4444 (USA & Canada)
fax: 812 355 4082

To Maria, my loving wife, all my children,
my sister-in-law Catherine, my brothers,
my sisters—all my relatives and friends.

Contents

Photographs

Forward

The turbulent 60s, the 9-11 disaster, the Iraq war, earthquakes, storms, and floods constantly disturb the impatient mind, causing many to search for answers. Lives are overwhelmed with endless conflicts. We are fragile mortals at the mercy of continuous and unpredictable calamities.

There are many words penned by the poets that provide precious moments of solace in order to escape to that place that gives most needed precious peace.

The poet, Zishan Evans, is no different. Here, in this collection of verses and lyrics, you will experience love and hate, victory and defeat, hope and helplessness, along with many inspiring and uplifting words of relevance.

My hope is that you will enjoy this diverse book of verses and lyrics and keep this book close by, to call on whenever there is desire for a burst of quick inspiration.

A Few Words From Zishan Evans

I am a romanticist, a dreamer,
    a positive thinker.
I see the world as a place to
    flourish and to do better.
I am sure, we are here to love
    and to be loved.

Love is what I look for
    in a sea and sky and star.
Love is what I look for
    in all the things that are.

I was born and reared on Chicago's great South side. I attended
Chicago's Grammar school and high school and
earned a college degree in Chicago. I currently live and work in
Northern California.

The Search for a Savior

When those innocent childhood days take flight
And adulthood, with its ache, comes to view,
We awake to misery, fear, and blight,
Where happiness ascends upon the few.

Encircled by savagery and endless strain
Controlled by elders, who do as they may,
Sharing not that good life, but whirling pain.
For this we sing, we dance, we scream, and we pray.

We cry to the invisible above.
Ah! The real truth we fail to understand
Is the power of hugs, enclosed by love,
With sweet kisses and a touch of a hand.

This joy, above all else for sure exists,
Is a loving savior within our midst.

It's Great to Be High Class

It's great to be high class
To be unlike the mass,
Imbued with style and grace,
Adorned with tail and lace.

It's great to be high class
To be unlike the mass,
Chosen not just for show,
Extolled for what we know.

Within this complex world of ours,
Our class lives in ivory towers.
Those who covet our success,
Adopt our manners and our dress.

It's great to be high class,
To be unlike the mass,
Full of ability,
With brains for all to see.

The Web

Suddenly as the insect falls,
Into the Web the spider spins,
The thread of horror quickly surrounds it.
The sting of death brings a sudden end.
But, oh that web the big folks spin
The pains of black folks' life begin.

Love Is What I Look For

(Dedicated to the family and friends of Faith).

You may keep your position, with all its pomp and class.
You may keep your ivory towers and separate from the mass.
But I'll hold onto my childlike view of love, life, and joy.
And seek an understanding with every man,
Woman, girl, and boy.

Love is what I look for along life's street.
Love is what I look for in ev'ry-one I meet.
Friends, they may be rich or poor,
And the color of their skin
Doesn't worry me at all.
I only look for beauty from within.

Love is what I look for in children at play.
Love is what I look for in darkness and in the day.
Let the seasons come and go
And whatever they may bring,
I will always cherish those that will make me smile,
Make my life worthwhile,
Never cause me pain,
And make me fall in love each day all over again.

Love is what it look for in sea and sky and star.
Love is what I look for in all the things that are.

To See You Again

To see you again,
To see you again,
To see you again is so grand.

Love has wings,
My heart sings
Loud and clear,
"I love you, dear."

To hold you again,
To hold you again,
Never more in vain is divine.
And I pray
Let me stay
In your arms
Close to your charms.

We shout to the world,
"World, we are lovers.
Giving each other joy,
Forsaking all others."
Darling

To see you again,
To see you again,
To see you again is so grand.
Love has wings,
My heart sings
Loud and clear,
"I love you, dear."

Where Lies Beauty

When the sun shines with piercing light
Bringing the bright day into my sight,
When I see birds flying and flowers everywhere
I ask myself is beauty there?

When the rainbows hover over the sky
And drops of rain touch my eye,
Is this beauty that brings such joy?
Or must I concede this to a grandiose ploy?

When I see kids on graduation day
And anxious brides making their way.
When babies evoke their maiden cries
This must be where beauty lies.

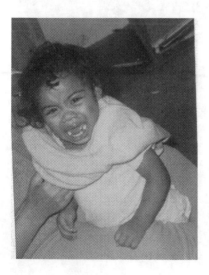

Babies

(From the mouth of a teenager).

Babies are fun and good to see
When others have them, but not me.

I love to cuddle one, now and then,
And hug it closer to my chin.

This joy, I cherish with much glee
As long as having it is not me.

Oh! Love!

Oh! Love! Bind our hearts, make them secure
And say strongly, our love is for sure.
Lets avoid all the fire, we could face,
While on the road that lovers embrace.

Oh! My Love! Will you always be true,
When you say every word, I love you.
Kindle our spirits and hearts and bind
As the stars look down on us and shine.

If you would reach out and hold my hand
Whispering sweet words, it would be grand.
Oh! My dear! Lay your head close to mine.
Hug me and keep our bodies entwined.

Leave me on the path of lasting peace.
Love is the reason joy will increase.
Say you love me, under the sky above.
Let's shout to the world our endless love.

Ah! Bobby!

(On the death of a Kennedy)

From the wild whirlwind, John sprang refreshing life.
Denying leisure and ease, even as
The mightiest kings, a vivacious wife
And fury, he flung hope's tight door ajar.
With eloquence he stood a deadly blow.
Then came his copy, emulative glow.
Too bold, he had a noble seed to sow.
Oh No! One cannot say he did not know,
Although rich love and time gives remedy
For that injurious sweet soul. His time,
As John's, Malcolm's, and King's is plain to see,
Is destined far beyond the fate of crime.
Ah! Bobby, with a will as firm as steel,
Only your kind is fair game for the kill.

I'm Black in the Ghetto

I'm black in the morning when I jump out of bed,
I'm black at noon when the sun is high above my head.
I'm black in the evening when my folks go to bed,
I'm black at midnight when I bow my head.

All my life, I've tarried in a peaceful way.
Meek and kind, I've sung songs of a better day.
I've even prayed that big folks mend their way.
But Oh! I'm black in the ghetto, where things
     don't change that way.

"Get down on your knees and pray!" I've heard the preacher say.
"There is a brighter day ahead; it's just around the way."
"Turn the other cheek. God will protect you," he'd say.
But, Oh! I'm black in the ghetto, where things
     don't change that way.

Oh, black woman, lift your head up high.
Your love consoles me.
Even your black beauty makes me sigh.
Your tears make me see.

Riots came after the man of peace they slayed.

"Aid the Black folks, Kill the Black folks," many said.
"Love-your-enemy," I heard fat leaders say.
But, Oh! I'm black in the ghetto where things
     don't change that way.

To a Hip Revolutionary

(From the mouth of a racist)

Dammit Boy!
How could you scare the pants off our asses!
We were good to you.
We give you welfare,
A.D.C.,
Job corps,
Mental-health clinics and
The county hospital.
Hell boy! How could you?
We gave you the G.I. bill,
Automotive schools,
Automation schools,
Junior colleges, and
Teachers' colleges.

Ungrateful fool, we gave you Teaching jobs,
Post Office jobs,
Civil Service jobs,
Transit jobs,
Social Worker jobs,
Community Worker jobs,
Crossing Guarded jobs,
Urban Renewal jobs,
Urban Progress jobs,
Urban This and Urban That jobs.

Come now boy. How could you talk all that revolutionary
        crap and hoard all those GUNS.
Surely, you planned to use them.
Negro, we had to stop you!

Yes! We knew just how.
We knew you were a PART TIME, loud mouth revolutionary—
    the type that talks trash during the day, sleeps at night,
    and posts no guards.
Ha! Ha! Ha! Young idiots!
We came safely in your neighborhood, down your alley,
    and up your street.
We easily surrounded your fortress. Fortress????????????
You bet we came in like lightning.
Boy! We raised hell.
We got you baby.
Black revolutionary, Black nationalist, Black this and Black that.
A negro ain't — -
Note: Don't get mad, get smart.

About Fred Hampton

(A Black Panther).

He was a trumpet,
Loud and clear.
He was a voice for RIGHT.
He talked, as others talked,
About the WRONG in America's society.
He wanted what all Black folks want,
To be really a part of America.
He was not a RAPIST, or a MURDERER, nor a THIEF.
Yes, he was GUNNED down by the State Attorney's POLICE.

Helplessness

The dreaded storm roared, crushing mercilessly
My home, the only treasure I possess.
Pain and suffering struck swiftly, is not gone.
Instantaneously, my vital job was blown.

Why, I shout, should I be selected for dread,
When others have a better life instead?
How was I picked by the power from above,
Distorting the meaning of joy and love?

I left for that place where bliss, one time, I had.
The happiness brought hugs from Mom and Dad.
Overcame by kisses from all the kids of mine.
Immediately, the world enhanced its shine.

I lowered my head in shame, but deep respect,
For believing now fate could be better yet.

The Journey

Overwhelmed by sorrow as goals in life fail,
While jobs evade you and a home is impossible to nail,
Sickness comes crashing and slams you to the floor,
Old creepy age rallies at your door.

You holler out loud to the heavens, in vain,
To intervene, to turn around your state,
To restore your hope, to comfort your brain,
To retrieve your dream, and curb your pain.

Finally, you turned to Mom and Dad
and those little ones you had,
The sibling that's near the heart,
And the few friends who share your spark.

These are those who love you most,
Who'll ease the journey to your final post.

Then I Found You

Reaching outward to seek the good life,
while drifting day by day, avoiding strife.
Dreaming of happiness through the year,
hoping to find an escape from fear.
Creeping close to the bottomless pit,
grasping a dream near the end of my wit.
Pressing on in a world full of gloom,
knowing that my path could lead to doom.
I lost my way. But then I found you.
Soon a heavenly place came into view.
Consumed by love and thrust in a trance,
suddenly I found the joy of romance.
What then are the words for me to say,
but I love you more each and every day?

The Road to Where

I watch the clock as it tick tick ticks.
It measures the distance without a glitch.
My life is running out with every passing hour.
Oh! I cry out for some staying power.

I remember how joyful those babies' cries,
The youthful years and the college good-byes.
Work has its merits allowing me to cope.
The church provides meaning and a great deal of hope.

While looking to the heavens, I stare into space.
I'm traveling toward an uncertain place.
Time takes its toll, as I drift day by day.
Where do I go from here? Where do I stay?

The end of my journey can explode lightning fast.
Without a road map, it may depend on my past.

Black Is Beautiful

Oh, Jet woman from the Ebony realm,
With a regal splendor and captivating charm,
Who art thou?

BLACK IS BEAUTIFUL to see,
Beautiful as anyone can be.
Solomon, the wise man, never could explain it,
How the Queen of Sheba filled them with delight.
When his heart could not resist her spell,
Solomon had these wise words to tell,
"Black is so enchanting,
Black is so romantic,
BLACK IS BEAUTIFUL,
Like the velvet of the night."

And Caesar, with his mighty pow'r,
Gave his heart up to the magic of this raven, lovely flow'r.
He dreaded the days he'd be without her charms,
And at night he dreamed he held her in his arms.

BLACK IS BEAUTIFUL to see,
And celestial more than blue can be.
All the stars at night twinkle in the blackness.

BLACK IS BEAUTIFUL, so beautiful,
BLACK IS BEAUTIFUL, so beautiful to see,
And rest your eyes, and rest your eyes upon.

On Love

Wandering helplessly through this worldly maze,
Crushed and shaken as cries to the heavens fade,
Abandoned by the invisible one we praise,
Knowing we have given our all, we turn to love.
Seeing love that's scattered and glowing from above,
Shifts our thoughts, tears from our eyes withdraw. Meanwhile,
Although our heart is slashed and wounded, we smile.
Convincing ourselves that love is not a ploy,
We cry out to love, remain and spread your joy.
Sweet love, we shout out, don't leave us. You must stay!
You're all we've got. We need you every day.
Oh! Love! That is always dear,
Give us peace and destroy our fear.

Together

Here we gather together to fight,
To change the world and make it right,
To seek Freedom and Peace that's fair,
To make a land all men can share.

Here we gather together for right,
Men of all nations, Black and White,
To save mankind from sin and shame,
To tarry on till victory's gained.

Night after night
As I lay down,
I have visions of heaven
Here in our country,
Where all people
Of all races
Live together in peace
And happiness always.

Here we gather together to shout,
To sing the song of Freedom out,
To let all men know of our plight,
To march because our cause is right.

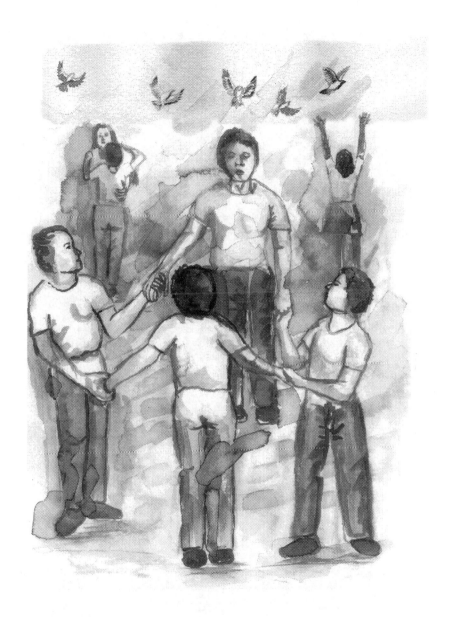

A Message of Comfort

(Dedicated to the family and friends of Juanita)

And even they, who love us most, slip away
To that mystic land we scarcely know. Lest
Some premonition of that fateful day,
Shake loose those fears that bit into the best
Of desperate souls and make them aware,
Their going leaves most lives in disarray.

Surely, if we could plan our day, they would fare
Far better who always manage to stay.
Yet life is thus. And death, greets us all.
But fret not. They would wish it so. Rather,
Look at the love of yesterday and recall
Those precious moments, love blooms together.
O! Sweet glorious love, that never dies,
Spark up life's journey till our day arrives.

Running Away from Pain

Running away from pain,
Looking for a reason to stay,
Wanting to return to that happy day,
Wishing old sadness would go away.

Running away from pain,
Traveling that road were dreamers go,
Hitching a ride on a rainbow sky,
Watching the rain as the breeze blows by.

Love should find ways to smile,
To make a beautiful life worthwhile.
Clinging to one that's sweet,
Enjoying the moments one meets.

Running away from pain,
Dreaming of those days shared with a flame,
Troubled by loneliness that won't mend,
Knowing now we've reached the lonely end.

The Two of You

(Grieving the loss of a loved one)

Where is that god you call to O sweet Shaw?
Is He in the sky where moon men pass by
Or perhaps mid the deep where fishes lie?
When hope leaves you, cause He fails to appear
To soothe your pain, to bring something to cling.
Stop! The good book says His time is so near.
But, is it really He you are seeking?
Perhaps, you yearn peace and freedom from fears,
Surely, that is the essence of your quest,
And to escape the hurt of advanced years.
Yet, love, above all else, equals them best.
O beautiful ones, the most we can do
Is to share our love with the two of you.

Heartache Is the Name of the Game

Her bright eyes,
Sweet face,
Striking thighs,
Velvet grace
Caught me by surprise.
Big and cool, hard to fool,
She took me with her thing
Now heartache is the name of the game.

Her hip sway, sham bliss, sexy way,
Tender kiss, captured all my soul.
Groovy tune, way out mind,
She took me with her thing.
Now heartache is the name of the game.

Jazzy and proud, I'd
Conquered all, until she stole my jive.
She came out of that heart-breaking bag,
And left me fighting to survive.

Her blithe smile, charm bags,
Flirting style, shapely legs, broke my uptight plan.
Blues and bars, in parked cars,
She took me with her thing.
Now heartache is the name of the game.

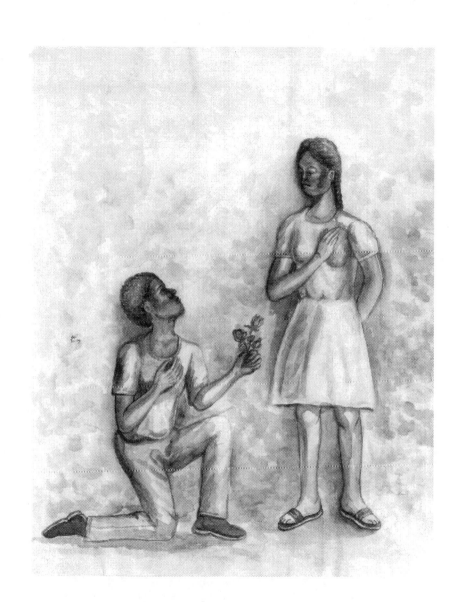

I Have To Know Where You're Coming From

I've tried to let you know a lot of things,
Most of the time you seem not to understand
And I suppose what makes it hurt so much
Is so many times, I don't know where you're at.
I have to know where you're coming from.

I've tried to get things right for you and me
'Cause I said I'd have to be the only one.
I've wanted things to be right at the very start.
So there are some things we need to get straight.
I have to know where you're coming from.

At first it was just little petty stuff,
And all I wanted was for you to admit it,
So you would know that you could talk to me
And that our love was stronger than what'll come up.

So darling please don't try to fix things up,
By lying to me or leaving something out.
It's not that I don't love you very much.
It's just that I want to know just where I stand.
I have to know where you're coming from.

You Can't Listen to Your Heart at All

Every prudish family possesses its pride and its joy
They even try to mate their girl with a prudish boy.
You're Okay, you're wise and smart when you see their way; But,
woe on you, when you follow your heart!
You're decidedly wrong, they say.

You can't listen to your heart at all.
It may hurt you if you heed its call,
Even though it leads you to the one you love.
Love must always seek approval from above.

You can't listen to your heart at all.
Though it pains you when the darkness falls,
You must think of those who may review your choice.
Teenage love must always heed its elder's voice.

The endless pain that love brings
Changes the world we know,
And makes us grow up with things
To face life as we go.

You can't listen to your heart at all.
Though your love refuses to let it stall,
It can't change the custom of your family's way;
Young love must accept every word old folks say.

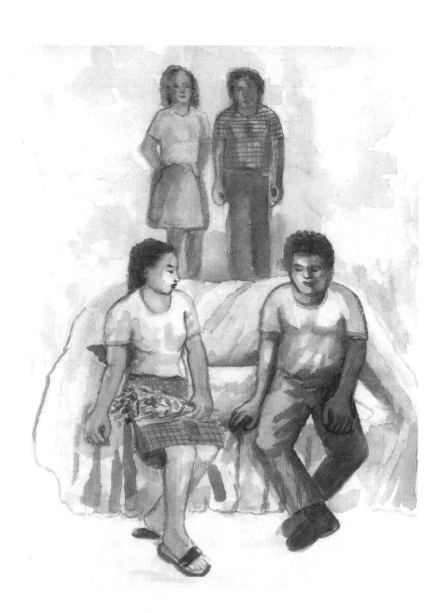

Oh, My Lord

Oh, My Lord
Oh, My Lord
Oh, My Lord
Oh, My Lord

No, no, no, no,
No, no, no, no,
How could she go?
We need her, so,
Oh, my Lord!
What are we really fighting for?

Oh, My Lord!
Oh, My Lord!
Oh, My Lord!
Oh, My Lord!

Zetta

Life goes on, no one cares.
Hours seem endless since you said goodbye,
People pass, they don't know,
I'm so lonely that I could cry.

Zetta, Zetta, oh, my love,
The hours I spent with you are gone.
I stay awake from dusk to dawn.
Zetta though you never stayed.
Your picture in my mind will never fade.

The orange color of fall,
The winter's blanket of snow,
The robin's music of spring,
And summer's cheerful glow,
They keep your beauty in my memory alive,
And in my dreams I wonder,
Could our love revive?

Zetta, Zetta, life is strange.
Because you gave me every sign,
You made my future seems so fine.
Yet you left me, my one world bereft me,
Zetta, Zetta, my Zetta.

A Review of Zetta, a 3-Act Play with Music by Zishan Evans

Every playwright from Euripides to Tennessese Williams has recognized the fact that conflict is the very stuff of effective drama—the one indispensable ingredient.

Zishan Evans, author of Zetta, has learned the lesson well. In this 3-act play with music, there is no end of conflict until the very end—when a gun in the hands of a misguided zealot resolves the multiple conflicts that have gone before.

While the agonizing and soul-searing conflict between blacks and whites provides the prevailing theme of the play, it is but one of a number of themes that keep Zetta moving along at a skillfully-measured pace to its final, heartbreaking resolution. Several correlated conflicts are woven into the fabric of the drama: the diametrically-opposed attitudes and morals of today's middle-aged parents and their children; the endless confrontation between entrenched authority and those who challenge the power and credentials of the establishment; the raging debate between those who would change our system by unbridled violence and those committed to peaceful, more patient means.

Set in the seething 60s, all these conflicts are played out on a black-and-white checkerboard across which Mr. Evans moves his characters with a high degree of compassion and skill.

Zetta, an 18-year old black girl with an Afro hair-do and views to match, is in painful conflict with her parents. Unlike them, she considers herself black on the inside as well as the outside. While she genuinely loves her mother and father, Zetta also loves a man whom they firmly disapprove of. In the hands of a less imaginative playwright, the man would be white; in this case, he is black—too black indeed to suit Zetta's conservative, affluent parents.

Zetta's father, George Mingo, is a successful attorney who has made it the hard way, but made it good. As a pillar of the black community and an aspiring candidate for the City Council, he doesn't want to rock the boat. Zetta's mother, Martha Mingo, whose great grandparents were white, has understandably mixed feelings. While she wants nothing more than to see her talented daughter happy, Martha is no more anxious to make waves than is her husband.

Malcome Clover, Zetta's lover, is more than anxious to rock the boat; he wants to overturn it. An impoverished and radical college student, he has no patience with racial tokenism or human Oreo Cookies. Dedicated to black separation, Malcolme is convinced that the only way to achieve long overdue justice for the black race is through controlled militancy.

Thus the battle is joined, then seemingly resolved. In a touching love scene, during which Zetta and Malcolme join hearts and voices in "Without Your Love," one of the plays ten engaging songs, they agree to marry after her imminent graduation from high school.

The play's shocking and climactic action takes place during a meeting of the Midtown Human Rights Association, at which Zetta is awarded the Association's annual Human Rights Scholarship Award.

What's the Use of Loving

What's the use of loving if it leads you to despair?
What's the use of hoping when you see the danger there?
I cannot change the fate that's dictated from above.
I cannot change my heart nor can I escape your love.

What's the use of loving if the end is plain to see?
What's the use of caring when it only troubles me?
Everyone will make mistakes in spite of what one knows.
Everyone must face one's plight and then one's fears will show.

When darkness falls,
The melodies of my heart call
For one love that's dear
And stillness that never comes near.

What's the use of loving if you cannot change your fate?
What's the use of planning, when you're sure it is too late?
Life goes on with all its pain and sorrow through the years.
Love is left to reap the tears from all the songs we hear.

I Miss Her When the Sun Goes Down

All I have left is a memory of her,
Deep down in my soul, she clings.
When I retire, my heart beats wildly for her.
It's over, it's over her voice rings.

I miss her when the sun goes down.
I worked hard through the day so gay.
My woman, she has left our town.
I can't face the things people say.

I miss her when the sun goes down
That woman, whom I love so well.
At midnight, when my love comes down
She sends me into a crying spell.

I'd travel all the way to the moon,
If I knew that she'd be there,
And sing out loud a heavenly tune
To let her know that I care.

I wake up at night with the blues,
In the night when the sun is down.
'Cause that woman I hate to lose.
I miss her when the sun goes down.

There's Something Within

There's something within
That brings back the dreams we once shared.
Your memory pounds in my brain
The sound of your name.

There's something within
That makes me feel you still care,
And though you are gone from me,
The joys I yet share.

But when I look for you,
Oh, my love,
Night begins to fall,
And darkness hides your face.

There's something within
That makes me believe you'll return.
Oh, darling, I wait for you to come back to me.

Standing in My Way

Am I number one or two?
How can I tell?
What can I do?
He says I'm the only one,
But he's a man, so that accounts for that.

Standing in my way is that man.
Crazy would I be to meet his plan.
He's as proud as he can be, knowing he has conquered me.
Lord knows I love him so,
But how I wish I could let him go.

Standing in my way is that man.
I can't help but follow his command.
I do wonder how I'd fair
When that man's not in my hair?
If I could just escape, I'd go away,
But my heart says nay.

I should leave him for another,
And go my merry way.
But how can I be sure
That all men aren't the same old way?

Standing in my way is that man.
In his arms he hugs me all he can.
How can I resist his charm,
When my love for him is warm?
Lord, I'll go to my grave with that man
Standing in my way.

I'm Trapped

I'm trapped in her web—
The sting I feel paralyzes my soul.
The pain I feel within
Sends my heart in a spin.

I'm trapped in her web—
I can't turn around, I can't go anywhere,
Can't see the light of day
But I'm happy this way.

My baby teases me with all her charm,
As she gives me all her loving
From night to morn.

I'm trapped in her web—
I'm just her prey,
Caught up in her spell.
Why don't I break away?
'Cause I'm so trapped, I stay.

The Last Dreams

Happiness and joy, a love, a prayer,
Food, wares, expensive things found everywhere.
Unsavory living saved by endless dreams,
While the real world stands full of pain and schemes.
A home, in the city, a car, and a van,
Waiting to be picked up by those who can.
Child in college, tuituion fully paid,
A wish unfulfilled, a heart that's dismayed.
There were many dreams before, some happy some sad.
The memories of good dreams were always glad.
Old nasty age roared out, the time is near.
The eyes close as the dreams disappear.

Peggy Taylor

(A friend to us all)

I know Peggy and her smile,
A serious soul but sometimes mild.
She would often question you,
Challenging the many things we do.

There were days she felt sad
Because of goals not met as planned.
Time change is always there
And a happier Peggy was everywhere.

Some say she's gone away.
It may be so, for that great day
Her spirits of love remain.
She moves to a place without pain.

Oh! When we cease our grief
And go back to our usual way,
Images of Peggy's bright light
Will always keep her in our sight.

Without Your Love

Without your love
Life is so lonely.
When the shadows of night appear
I wish you were here.

Without your love
My sorrow's endless,
And my tears make me feel so blue
Just thinking of you.

Oh, darling won't you return to me,
'Cause darling, I'll always yearn to be
Close to you dear.

Without your love
Life has no meaning,
And the joy that I hoped we'd share
Is no longer there
Unless you care
And swear by stars above
I'll never be without your love.

Harold

(A husband, a father, a brother, a friend)

Harold was fragile, full of joy and hope.
He traveled the road that good folks take.
Suddenly, awake and not, with a silent heartache,
He drifted on a dreaded path with which he could not cope.

Afraid of that place he knew little of.
A plight not planned but sanctioned from above.
Surrounded by those who treasure him best
Loving faces, caring hands, and prayers that bless.

Kind words that often relieve a desperate soul,
Gave solace and peace with grasping hope,
While edging closer to that final toll
On a day uncertain and a place remote.

Oh! But we who remain! must cherish his life
And remember the good times he shared
With his friends, family, and wife.

The Magic of Two

What is this life without another?
It's like a newborn baby without a mother,
Or stuck on a precipice, no one's near,
Or entering a forest with all its fear.

What is this life, if you are not mine?
An empty place, a dungeon, where one is confined.
How can I go on without your smile,
When your thrilling embraces make life worthwhile?

Heaven is just a place, if you aren't there.
But oh! What a place, if we are a pair.
There is magic, when two are entwined,
Just you and me, and sweet berry wine.

When I close my eyes, I see you.
Then I know the magic of two.

Happiness

Happiness is elusive and hard to find.
It's mostly with someone else, time after time.
I search endlessly, in many ways.
If it comes, it goes. It seldom stays.

I often dream happiness will come one day.
But it rarley makes it, leaving me to pray.
Pain and suffering seem to never end.
I wait for happy times to begin.

What should I ask of the mighty one
When happiness finds no place in my life?
Should I cry out louder and holler for some
Miracle to spring swiftly within my sight?

Oh! My happiness, where are you now?
I long to claim and hold you, somehow.

If I Have You

What would life be if I have you?
Extraordinary, but surely true,
Heaven is wherever you are.
Together we'll follow our star.

The world would be a place to soar,
Knowing you are mine and I am yours.
I marvel at the vast sky above
But nothing is greater than our love.

I wish to hold you in my arms forever.
Your warmth and beauty is all I see.
Would I leave you for another? Never!
Happiness is destined for you and me.

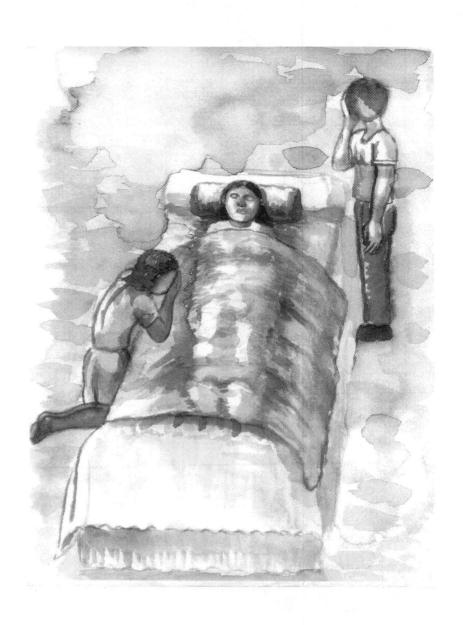

The Last Good-Bye

(Dedicated to the family of Dreina Mayfield)

Her words were soft and gentle.
The conversation, with laughter and gestures,
Was about little things,
Everyday things,
Things for tomorrow and beyond.
A painless future,
Full of hope and excitement,
Surrounded us.
Finally, we looked each other in the eyes,
With a smile and a touch of the hands,
We parted and went our separate ways.

The morning came, with the sun exceedingly bright,
Spreading joy.

It was at work, I heard the news.
She is dead.
She died in her bed.

A shock, a chill,
A cry of disbelief hovered everywhere.
Oh! Our fagile dreamer has passed on
To that mystical place of endless nights,
Of silence, of painless plight.

Good-Bye
O' Beautiful Dreamer
O' Wonderful Spirit of Hope.

Misery

Crossing the train tracks without a gate
The train paid no attention and did not wait.
All the pain of the world flashed before his eyes,
The drive-by shootings and the many suicides.

Cancer, shared with heart attacks, diabetes, and strokes
Allows no mercy to bad or good folks.
Bombings, hangings, stabbings, stonings, and burning alive,
A nightmare affecting too many people world wide.

Bacteria, virus spreading everywhere alike.
Don't forget the poison that settles a fight.
Motorcycles, cars, boats, and flying in a plane.
Takes your life or runs you down and leaves you lame.

Floods, volcanoes, earthquakes, the great acts of God.
Unstoppable disasters in a world that's odd.
A vision of a new world consumed his brain
As the lights faded and the end gently came.

From "Zetta," a 3-Act Play with music by Zishan Evans

Published in 1989 by Bird International Group

We must stand together
as one, or we will fall together separately.

> O, oppressed and valiant sons!
> Speak out for better days!
> The test of eternity runs
> Through the maze of a thousand ways
> To measure the mettle of man.

All the people who make peace are people who love peace,
but not all the people who love peace are peacemakers.
We need peacemakers, not peace-lovers who do nothing.
What is the difference? The difference is in the basic approach.
The peacemaker gets prominently, personally involved,
righting what has been wronged, uniting what has been separated,
while peace-lovers avoid getting into the fray
for the sake of "keeping the peace."

Songs by Zishan Evans
(words and music)

Standing in My Way
I'm Trapped
Heartache is the Name of the Game
I Have to Know Where You're Coming From
There's Something Within
Zetta
It's Great to be High Class
Love is What I Look For
You Can't Listen to Your Heart
Together
To See You Again
I'm Black in the Ghetto
Without Your Love
Black is Beautiful
Oh! My Lord

Other Works by Zishan Evans:
"Zetta," a 3-Act Play with Music

Printed in the United States
By Bookmasters